ALSO BY MARY RUEFLE

Selected Poems

Mary Ruefle

SELECTED POEMS

WAVE BOOKS Seattle and New York

Published by Wave Books

www.wavepoetry.com

Wave Books titles are distributed to the trade by
Consortium Book Sales and Distribution
Phone: 800-283-3572 / SAN 631-760x

Library of Congress Cataloging-in-Publication Data
Ruefle, Mary, 1952–
[Poems. Selections]
Selected poems / Mary Ruefle.—1st ed.
p. cm.
ISBN 978-1-933517-45-2 (hardcover : alk. paper)
I. Title.
PS3568.U36A6 2010
811'.54—dc22
2010005808

Poems from *The Adamant, Cold Pluto, Post Meridian, Among
the Musk Ox People, Tristimania, Indeed I Was Pleased with
the World* appear with the permission of Carnegie Mellon
University Press, www.cmu.edu/universitypress

Poems from *Apparition Hill* appear with
permission from CavanKerry Press, Ltd.

Designed and composed by Quemadura
Printed in the United States of America

9 8 7 6 5 4 3 2 1

FIRST EDITION

CONTENTS

I found it, and alas, it was utterly restored

WALTER PATER

Selected Poems

Standing Furthest

All day I have done nothing.
To admonish me a few aspen
jostle beneath puny stars.
I suppose in a rainforest
a draft of hands brought in
the tubers for today, women
scratched their breasts in the sunlight
and smiled: someone somewhere
heard the gossip of exotic birds
and passed it on in the night
to another, sleeping curled like an ear:
of all things standing furthest
from what is real, stand these trees
shaking with dispensable joy,
or those in their isolation
shading an extraordinary secret.

Transpontine

Though the little wooden bridge in May
still joins—
I can't distinguish my finest memory
from among the worthless.
Now and then there are bare trees
between gray towns,
and soot rising in pink air.
With a rare tenderness
I have dispersed all agreement.
I need no mediator.
No trees to surround the shelter,
no sky to extend a hand to the trees,
hardly that of a life to accept its claptrap
unity: for as surely as I am drawn
toward a beaming uncertainty,
a cavity of earth will open
and the dreadful hoot of a bird
be absorbed:

There's you, laughing:
the abysmal repeats itself.
You are not yet dead,
I am already alone.

Replica

You've wasted another evening
sitting with imaginary friends,
discussing the simplest possible
arrangement of an iris.
The sky, too, like a delicate dress
streaked with bleach, has been thrown away.
Once you wanted to be someone else
or another thing altogether: an iris in April,
or only its pistil, just that, a prayer so small
it was only rumored. What can it matter?
You know now your own life doesn't belong to you,
the way a child defects into his childhood
to discover it isn't his after all.
Still, on this and other evenings,
only another replica of thoughts
has been lost:
your life has its own, intact, far distant,
and unknowingly you have devoted your lives
to each other:

at Izura, toward dawn,
someone walks down to the sea
astonished you have taken so long.

The Intended

One wants so many things . . .
One wants simply, said the lady,
to sit on the bank and throw stones
while another wishes he were standing
in the Victoria and Albert Museum
looking at Hiroshige's *Waterfall*:
one would like to be able to paint
like that, and Hiroshige wishes
he could create himself out of the
Yoro sea spray in Mino province where
a girl under the Yoro waterfall wants
to die, not quite sure who her person is,
but that the water falls like a sheet of tin
and another day's thrown in the sieve:
one can barely see the cherry blossoms
pinned up in little buns like the white hair
of an old woman who was intended for this hour,
the hour intended to sit simply on the bank
at the end of a long life, throwing stones,
each one hitting the water with the *tick* of
a hairpin falling in front of a mirror.

From Memory

The old poet riding on horseback in winter
came face-to-face with a thief who had
beaten his horse to a pulp. Once and for
all, they recognized each other without
speaking; one held a bright knife to the
other's throat while the other offered the
bleeding velvet of his animal to show that
he, too, had smuggled his life through
every conceivable hour.

Patient Without an Acre

Look how appropriately incomplete
I am: I never carry a pocket mirror.
My skin takes the light.
I don't know where it goes.
Maybe it passes right through me.
Maybe it follows me,
making me easy to follow,
for there's no mistaking
what it is: a life all right,
and my own, but to what end?
I can't work, much less love.
Love, there's no mistaking the word
for it: once you've driven the
wild breath in, you'll have
a little glass hammer,
perfectly useless. This,
the flint of all things!
They say one off another
we light our way with
what's been lit for us.
While my own dark risk
is not to grow, not
until I've given myself to a leper,
until he's touched my soul with his body

and together we work like the missing part
of a crossword.
Work, of which I wasn't able!
Love and work. *Lieben, Arbeiten.*
The little glass hammer is ringing!
There's another word for work
another word for love
a language with one word for both
and a country with no words at all.
Look at the men and women
unable to understand:
there are two of them walking
alone and in love
coming back from the fields
that have bent them.

All the Activity There Is

Morning and raining,
raining and morning,
the first soft ashes
of light hit the boathouse
again and again:
all the muffled horns
on a faraway highway
blowing the dice of lights
like coals in your hands:
see, see,
see how sorrow can
derange a man's mind.

Barbarians

Here and there, between trees,

cows lie down in the forest

in the midafternoon

as though sleep were an idea

for which they were willing

to die.

Perfume River

She thinks fishing is an odd way
to make love: watching her husband rooted
in water, slick to the hips under the arch
of a bridge, his whole rod nodding
like hart's-tongue fern in its youth.
She has other thoughts hidden
inside of these, barely visible
like the stamens of crocus.

Ah spring! The cedar waxwing with a plume
in his ass, pumping seeds from his mouth
like a pinball machine.

Palaver of scents
and the boys standing naked under the waterfall.
Pachinko! The word enters her bloodstream:

Holy Mary mother of God-who's-gone-fishing-today,
she'll stay out bog-trotting until she's
blue in the face, like an orchid.

At the North Pole

More hopelessly than in the first dream
you walked away . . .
but through what streets
I do not know
since it is no longer a question
of architecture
in my city of dreams,
where meetings, vague encounters,
even glances
topple like rubble in a tropical storm:

Perhaps there are only paths of weather
after all,
all weathers and a crossroads
where heaven police
let the palm that will save you
enter the blizzard that will kill you
so that the whole world
shall see it singled out,
lonely and planted in a white swirl.
Either the city is so small
or the palm so enormous
that in any case
it fills it completely.

The Beautiful Is Negative

What is to be made of this custom:
piercing the eyes of a bird
so that it may sing better?
You ask me that! Paul, this is
the twentieth century: trouble is real.
Deer polish their antlers
on fruit trees, like a girl
polishing apples on her hair.
Don't be a fly wringing his hands
as though worry could save the world.
What's wrong with the world?
Human hair hung from the lowest limb
will keep out the deer.
This is the animal kingdom, where
danger is clear and the tree grows
out of itself like an antler
butting the air—
huge, inexpressible growth!
Boys, girls, say sincerely
what you would like to become:
thighs shining like braided bread
in the grass,
or crickets scraping away
when words fail you?

The Last Supper

It made a dazzling display:
the table set with the meat
from half of a walnut, a fly
on a purple grape, the grape
lit from within and the fly
bearing small black eggs.
We gathered round the oval table
with our knives, starved
for some inner feast.
We were not allowed to eat,
as we had been hired as models
by the man at our head.
Days passed
in which we grew faint with hunger.
Later we were told
that although we did not appear
on the canvas
our eyes devouring these things
provided the infinite light.

Pen and Ink

The important thing is not to get depressed.
Why, I am certainly no drunkard, nor a
spendthrift. I am a regular German
in my behavior.

The doctor visiting Chekhov, who spat blood
on his bed, was called by a crude phone
to go at once and treat Tolstoy,
whose intermittent heartbeats
were signaling for help. Now
if it were not for the doctor
I think I might start drinking
if you told me this tale.

But imagine his joy,
riding between commitments
along the coast of Yalta
in the fresh open air!

Depicted on a Screen

I hear over in China
people break a willow branch
whenever they say goodbye.

My mind is no longer serene.
Late April and the willow,
already yellow, is broken

with snow. Roadside daffodils
are tearing their sleeves, but
lightly, with the semiconfidence

of someone shrieking in a movie.
I eat popcorn like tiny pieces
of crumpled paper.

The words dissolve
on my tongue.
I know this world up and leaves

on a lacquered palanquin,
taking with it a splendor
I won't see again.

But the gods will go with me
if I put myself in their path.
How is it done?

All of the heroes
you see falling down
were filmed trying to stand up.

Heaven on Earth

My heaven will be spent on earth
up until the end of the world.

SAINT THÉRÈSE OF
LISIEUX (1873–1897)

i

You know, Mother, I have always wanted to be a saint. Ever since
Celeste held up a basket of dress scraps, crying "Here my little sis-
ter, *choose!*" And I chose—*all*. There are always children spinning
themselves into statues, having to choose in the terrible stillness
what am I before being able to move the enactment: had you not
brought me up so well, I would never have cried when choosing to be
his plaything.

ii

A hoop of no value, an even smaller ball—something he might lose,
nothing with a string. I beg to be *stolen*!

iii

Whenever the boys spoke to me, I hid my fingers in my muff and there
I would make small imitations of Christ. These little acts of love

formed a flower bud out of my face. Although I was barely fourteen, I felt it best to leave the world at once.

iv

What an interesting study the world becomes when one is ready to leave it: a skirt, a set of kitchen utensils, little parcels. The yellow shop on rue Demi-Lune where there's an éclair in the window waiting for *me*! And the libraries where I would have broken my head.

v

Now all my Sisters are sealed round the bed like a row of onions: vocation of the Carmelite, sister, spouse, mother, *warrior*; the priest and the doctor. I would that all of their torments were reserved for me. But I am too small to climb the stairs! I want to seek out a means of going to heaven by a little way, a way that is very straight, very short, and totally new. I want to ride *in an elevator*.

vi

Believe me, don't wait until tomorrow to begin becoming a saint. I oblige you to take your wooden tops and go play for *at least an hour* in the attic. I must stay here in my bed. I'm waiting for the Thief, you know.

vii

I wonder what he will do at my death to surprise me. Will he sip me up like a dewdrop? So, I'm already thinking that, if I am not surprised enough, I will pretend to be surprised just to please him.

viii

I'm suffering very much, it's true, but am I suffering well, that's the point. Take silence for example—what failures in clarity it prevents. I speak especially about silence because it's on this point that I fail the most.

ix

Are peaches in season? Are they selling plums in the street? Violets from a cart? Only in the kingdom of heaven will it no longer be necessary to have some *souvenir*.

x

No line has ever given me more pleasure to write than this one in which I have the good fortune to tell you he is very nearly through unpetaling me!

xi

They think I have difficulty in breathing! I am pretending to take little sips to let him know that I am drinking in his words.

xii

Scarcely had I laid my head on the pillow when I felt a bubbling stream on my lips. My blood was like a plaything. When God abandoned it, he fell asleep and dreamt he was still playing with it.

The Beginnings of
Idleness in Assisi

Mark how curious it is with him:
he would walk for days
in the same field, wearing
no more than a robe,
stooping now and then for
a sprig of woodruff.
His passion
was to be stung by a bee,
his body releasing its secret purpose
into the body of the bee, that
he might be done with it
once and for all. It took
his breath away, and
forever after he stood there
lonely as a finger: whatever
touched or hoped to touch,
whatever tried to count
the features of his profile
found only a thumbnail sketch.
Like this little tiger lily,
his new stance we never understood
with any human certainty.

Indeed, we ceased to believe in it.
Either he is letting go
all the animals at once
from his bosom, or welcoming
them one by one
into his arms:
the birds at his feet do not hold
his kindness against him,
chattering to one another that one day
he will come to his senses,
and sitting down, the whole
beautiful and weighted world
will settle in his lap
like the statue of a cat.

Lapland

The little Lapp girl wanders around picking cloudberries
while the bluethroat sings one of his hundred songs.
There are tiny white flowers, too: angelica,
and the wild white ranunculus.
The reindeer eat lichen and moss under the melting snow.
Some of the lichen are a thousand years old
and do not recognize the modern world.
The geography lessons are young in comparison,
though this one is older than most, since
Lapland lies on no map and the little Lapp girl
must be at least eighty by the looks of the book.
It is doubtful she remembers the day
of this photograph. The pencil-stroke of a birch
can be seen in the distance. Once in a while
she must still hear the bluethroat and think
of her childhood. Out of a hundred songs
he has not forgotten the one he sang
on an afternoon when the snow left and
the wild white ranunculus took its place.
But he is the peripheral sort
and not at the center of anything.

Diary of Action and Repose

In some small substation of the universe
the bullfrogs begin to puff out their mouths.
The night-blooming jasmine is fertilized
in the dark. I can smell it.
And then someone unseen and a little ways off
picks up his flute and asserts his identity
in a very sweet way.
I'll throw in the fact it's April in China—
ah exotica, soft night—
while the bullfrog, the jasmine, and the flute
form a diary of action that explains my repose:
spring, ripening to her ideal weight, has fallen
from the bough and into my lap.
For twenty minutes the world is perfect
while two or three thinks fumble for their glasses
in my cranium—
ah the impulse to hurt and destroy has arrived
and *oh* into pretty and endless strips it pares the place
round and round—

How It Is

Things begin to burgeon. The peas go gallivanting
in their pods. That old spring prop, birdsong, wafts
through the trees, the trees with their leaves lit
like the underside of the sea. We walk deep inside
and have a picnic there. In the filtered gloss of
the forest, pears come out of our pockets and
lunch proceeds. All this is pleasant and I will
erase it. I will erase it because the height of insanity
demands that I do. The height of insanity says we were
in a field under a festoon of clouds. The height of insanity
says I was not there. The height of insanity says
I have not had a happy life. The height of insanity
says it was snowing, insists that I say *in the heaven*
of February, in a porcelain snow. I will erase it.
The heaven of February knows I was there, in the woods
on the twenty-second of April, eating. My hand goes
to my mouth. There is horror in my eyes. How do I know?
The martinet in a boiled shirt says it is so.
Christ, I've had a happy life! But who am I to know?

Timberland

Paul's Fish Fry in Bennington, Vermont, is no longer
Closed For The Season Reason Freezin. The umbrellas
have opened over the picnic tables and the bees are
beginning to annoy the french fries, the thick shakes
and real malts of my past:

I am thirteen thousand miles removed, on the delta
of the Pearl River, eating a litchi. Its translucent flesh just
burst in my mouth; shreds of it glitter between my teeth.
I smile but the fruit seller is sour. In fact, he is so sour
the only man on earth he resembles is Paul. But the litchi . . .

Actually none of this has happened yet. I am nineteen
years old. I am riding in the boxcar of a freight train
hurtling toward Pocatello, Idaho. In a very dangerous move
I maneuver my way back to the car behind me, an open gondola
carrying two tons of timberland eastward out of Oregon:

it is here I will lie all night, my head against the logs,
watching the stars. No one knows where I am. My mother thinks
I am asleep in my bed. My friends, having heard of a derailment
at ninety miles an hour on the eastbound freight, think I am
dead. But I'm *here*, hurtling across the continent with un-

believable speed. We are red-hot and we go, the steel track
with its imperceptible bounce allows us to go, our circuitous
silhouette against the great Blue Mountains and my head in a
thrill watching the stars: I am not yet at a point in my life
where I am able to name them, but there are so many and they are

so white! I'm hurtling toward work at Paul's, toward the litchi-
bite in Guangzhou, toward the day of my death all right, but all
I can say is I am *happyhappyhappy* to be here with the stars and
the logs, with my head thrown back and then pitched forward
in tears. And the litchi! it's like swallowing a pearl.

Cul-de-sac

The milkman delivered the milk.
Out of desperation, I suppose.
My mother took her mink stole
out of its bag and I saw her initials
on the inside satin shimmering
like the future itself.
My father took his golf clubs out of their mitts
and I saw the enormous integers
each one was assigned.
In September I got new shoes
whether I needed them or not.
In April a hat of pastel straw.
We had a carport and lived on a cul-de-sac.
I know these things are fleshless and void,
as unimportant as a mouse.
Hardly full of the farmlight and yet like
the farmlight that slips in under my door
where my bookcases are weighted with books.
My brother has a van full of rifles,
a string of wives and children
along the interstate, and I do not know
if he shaves or does not. We each think
the other has flattened a life.
I read one day that Jesus had a sister.

I wish I had her tenacity.
The woodshed shudders in the wind.
The barn is stark on the hill.
My mother's name and my father's numbers
lie in a landfill that is leveled far away.
Brother, I have been unable to attain a balance
between important and unimportant things.

The Pedant's Discourse

Ladies, life is no dream; Gentlemen,
it's a brief folly: you wouldn't know
death's flashcard if you saw it.
First the factories close, then the mills,
then all the sooty towns shrivel up
and fall off from the navel.
And how should I know, just because my gramma
died in one? I was four hundred miles away,
shopping. I bought a pair of black breasts
with elastic straps that slip over the shoulder.
I'm always afraid I might die at any moment.
That night I heard a man in a movie say
I have no memories and presumably he meant it.
But surely it was an act. I remember my gramma's
housedress was covered with roses. And she
remembered it too. How many times she turned
to her lap and saw the machines: the deep folds
of red shirts endlessly unfolding while they dried.
Whose flashcard is that? So, ladies and gentlemen,
the truth distorts the truth and we are in it up
to our eyebrows. I stand here before you tonight,
old and wise: cured of vain dreams, debauched,
wayward, and haggard. The mind's a killjoy, if
I may say so myself, and the sun's a star,
the red dwarf of which will finally consume us.

Instrument of the Highest

CHAIM SOUTINE (1893–1943)

Ah the truth,
            is the rank lustful lives of men and women
            going after it
in all its *red*—

it is just this nipple exposed beneath the rag
                        puce with lava-milk,

it is just this beef-stink in the studio,
the popped-out eyes of rotting salmon,

a particular chicken: the scrawniest one in the shop,
                        long neck and blue skin

I'm going to hang it up by the beak with a nail.
In a few days it should be perfect.

It must be *very very* dead.
                        Even the red gladioli
have passed over into that garden where things shout

                    don't look at me!

Everything startled into still thinking

                                                it is alive.

What else is spirit but the hectic orifice

                                of the still unwilling
to admit they are excruciatingly gone?

                        A conniption fit of fact?

                                Still nothing new.
What is more beautiful than that?

Naked Ladies

Rousseau wanted: a cottage on the Swiss shore,
a cow, and a rowboat.

Stevens wanted a crate from Ceylon full of jam
and statuettes.

My neighbors are not ashamed of their poverty
but would love to be able to buy a white horse,
a stallion that would transfigure the lot.

Darwin was dying by inches from not having anyone to talk to
about worms, and the vireo outside my window wants nothing less
than a bit of cigarette-wool for her nest.

The unattainable is apparently rising on the tips of forks
the world over . . .

So-and-so is wearing shoes for the first time

and Emin Pasha, in the deepest acreage of the Congo,
wanted so badly to catch a red mouse! Catch one he did
shortly before he died, cut in the throat by slavers who
wanted to kill him. *At last!* runs the diary

and it is just this *at last* we powder up and call progress.

So the boys chipped in and bought Bohr a gram of radium
for his 50th birthday.

Pissarro wanted white frames for his paintings
as early as 1882, and three francs for postage, second place.

Who wants to hear once more the sound of their mother throwing
Brussels sprouts into the tin bowl?

Was it *ping* or was it *ting*?

What would you give to smell again the black sweetpeas
choking the chain-link fence?

Because somebody wants your money.

The medallions of monkfish in a champagne sauce . . .

The long kiss conjured up by your body in a cast . . .

The paradisiacal vehicle of the sweet-trolley rolling in
as cumulous meringue is piled on your tongue
and your eye eats the amber glaze of a crème brûlée . . .

The forgiveness of sins, a new wife, another passport,
the swimming pool, the rice bowl

full of rice, the teenage mutant ninja turtles escaping
as you turn the page . . .

Oh brazen sex at the barbecue party!

Desire is a principle of selection. Who wanted *feet* in the first place?

Who wanted to stand up? Who felt like walking?

Toward the Correction
of Youthful Ignorance

There was a carriage in the story and when it rumbled
over the cobblestones one caught a glimpse
of the gaslit face inside . . .

But the young men, after reading "The Dead"
by James Joyce, sauntered out of the classroom
and agreed: "it's *puerile*, that's what it is."

Are there no more mothers who lie yellowing
in their gowns? Am I to insist, when I hate my desk,
my galoshed legs shoved in under, and all
Christmas dinners right down to eternity—?

When I was younger I wandered out to the highway
and saw a car with its windshield beautifully cracked.
The blood on the seat was so congealed
and there was so much of it, I described it to no one.

When I was younger I did not think
I would live to see the cremation of my youth,
then the hair on my arms went up in flames
along with my love for Nelson Giles.

Now I saunter out in the lamblike snow
where the black squirrels leap from bough
to bough, gobbling everything.

The snowflakes are pretty in a way.
The young men know that and compact them into balls.
When they hit my windshield I begin to laugh.

I think they are right after all:
there's no love in this world

but it's a beautiful place.
Let their daughters keep the diaries,
careful descriptions of boys in the dark.

Trust Me

What can be discussed in words
I beg to state in brief.
A man has only one death:
it may be as light as goose down
or as heavy as a fatted hog.
Gingerly, the flowers open
and are crushed in the vat.
What's in your new perfume?
The hills of Africa are in it,
and the cormorants with their mouths full of fish,
a bed of carnations, a swannery in Switzerland,
the citrine sun baking Napa
and a rhino whining at the moon.
An after-dinner argument is in it
and the ever-stronger doses of claptrap
we are forced to take while still alive.
A whole aeroplane, wings and all,
and the lush spaghetti siphoned into lips
poised for a kiss.
Finish it, finish it.

Entirely, Eventually

The afternoon digresses into evening,
autumn into snow.
Tu Fu and Li Po met, and then they parted,
and who's to say which day was their digression?
Such poems of departure are not possible today:
we sail forward and fly back like a loving pair
of purple mandarin ducks.
Who leaves for the mountains and never comes back?
No one I know. I turned on the television
and there was a man on channel two
talking about perfume.
A man on channel three was lost in the mountains
and his dog kept smelling things.
After that I went over to the window
and was surprised to see it was light.
I thought of sleep, a major digression.
But I couldn't sleep. I kept thinking
about that man on the mountain.
After he made that movie I'm sure
he went home and made love to his wife.
And then maybe he ate some eggs.
But it breaks my heart to think
he is bound to lose the thread entirely,
eventually.

Nice Hands

I was born in a hospital. I stank.
They washed me. Five years later
my brain was a lightbulb that flickered on and off,
my soul was a milk bottle yearning to be full,
my stomach, made of concrete, had a long wooden table
where six dressed kittens sat, holding up their bowls.
Now my stomach has the pizzazz of a hundred colored bulbs
hanging by a wire over a cantina where someone in a white sheet
is learning to pour wine on the altar.
The cats have grown, scattered, multiplied
in my brain, where they fight over milk spilt
from the bottle, described now as an odalisque,
their cat hair standing on end.
And my soul is the concrete room
with an unstable card table where no one plays and nothing feeds,
though when I die there's always the chance
someone with nice hands will wash me.

Rain Effect

A bride and a groom sitting in an open buggy
in the rain, holding hands but not looking
at each other, waiting for the rain to stop,
waiting for the marriage to begin, embarrassed
by the rain, the effect of the rain on the bridal
veil, the wet horse with his mane in his eyes,
the rain cold as the sea, the sea deep as love,
big drops of rain falling on the leather seat,
the rain beaded on a rose pinned to the groom's
lapel, the rain on the bride's bouquet,
on the baby's breath there, the sound of the rain
hitting the driver's top hat, the rain
shining like satin on the black street,
on the tips of patent leather shoes, Hokusai's
father who polished mirrors for a living, Hokusai's
father watching the sky for clouds, Hokusai's father's son
drawing rain over a bridge and over the people crossing
the bridge, Hokusai's father's son drawing the rain
for hours, Hokusai's father rubbing a mirror, the rain
cold as the sea, the sea cold as love, the sea swelling
to a tidal wave, at the tip of the wave white.

Cold Pluto

The moon tonight—
those milky & sliding tears on the face of Christ
that hung in my grandmother's bedroom!
The purple wardrobe of his open heart!
My grandma & Crashaw, centuries apart, collide tonight
in a lunar spell.
My memory can be so gibbous. My brain the matted back
of an embroidered swatch of cloth. Mosquitos!
So many mosquitos in the eerie light!
I swat my arm, then suck the blood
for its salt. In the penetralia of my existence
there must be some marrow, not this glucose
of the virtuoso, the King of Collisions.
What I would give to see him dangling.
Despised. Out of power.
No one wants to live like this.
The crowd swells. Off with his head! Off
memory, off oeuvre, off with the stuff
atoms are made of! To live without him, to be dim,
to live under the incomparable spell of impossibly cold
Pluto. Aloof & severe. Impossibly,
but unfortunately, like the green glazed tiles
of a distant Chinese roof.

Out of a Hundred

The shadow on the wall vanished. The sun vanished,
a receding siren. The violet light that dressed the snow
vanished, and the steam, rising from the kettle
in a fabulous plume. A child vanished into muscle and speech.
I myself passed through the last locked gate
at the end of the tenth corridor
and stood very still while the prison-patch of memory
was sewn on my sleeve. My cap pulled low.
And then the question:
What did you bring? Was there not a moment, marched along
as I was, when I put out my finger and wiped some dust
from the wall, saved a dead fly, stole pollen from an Alpine
flower? I didn't know what to say.
Was there not a moment, in some forgotten corner, where beauty
still lingered, when you kept a piece of skin from the plum
you were peeling? No, I said.
No there was no moment
or no you did not? It was confusing, to say the least.
I could see that the course of history had changed.
Even if you knew that, you might not know
there are moments seized with tenderness.
This was one of them.

Merengue

I'm sorry to say it, but fucking
is nothing. To the gods, we look
like dogs. Still, they watch.
Did you lose your wallet?
Did you rip up the photo?
Did you pick up the baby
and kiss its forehead?
Did you drive into a deer?
Did you hack at the grass
as if it could kill you?
Did you ask your mother for milk?
Did you light the candles?
Did you count the buttons on your shirt?
Were you off by one? Did you start again?
Did you learn how to cut a pineapple,
open a coconut?
Did you carry a body once it had died?
For how long and how far?
Did you do the merengue?
Did you wave at the train?
Did you finish the puzzle, or save it for morning?
Did you say something? Would you repeat it?
Did you throw the bottle against the wall?
Did it break? Did you clean it up?

Did you tear down the web? What did you do
with the bug the spider was saving?
Did you dive without clothes into cold water?
Have you been born?
What book will you be reading when you die?
If it's a good one, you won't finish it.
If it's a bad one, what a shame.

silly

Topophilia

I was going to ardently pursue this day
but you know how these things go.
I am a Hun and the sun is my chieftain
and chieftains are as they appear to their Huns . . .
So, sunless, I go from being a sleepy angel wearing god's toga
to a woman in a bathrobe wandering around a well-appointed house.
The transformations are astonishing; like a birch in April
the blood rushes to my head, only it's not April
and all the signs say don't go too soon, don't go too far,
don't even pass. The birch stands still and these things
are of some consequence in the country. And a domineering
little bird has eaten all the seeds. I think one day
it will build its nest in my abandoned cranium.
I study nature so as not to do foolish things.
For instance, in the worst windstorms
only the most delicate things survive:
a vireo's nest intact on the lawn next to the roots
of a monstrous tree. Life makes so much sense!
There goes the coach. The coach is of real gold
and the new queen is in it. I like trips, I book them all,
and I'm one of the lucky: my memories are actually finer
than those of those who go. I suspect the queen is going
to the despot's private party where they shove sweetmeats
down your décolletage and have a goose so slowly roasted

the poor bird cries whenever you pull off a piece
and everyone shrieks with joy. What does the outer world
know of the inner? It's like listening to wolves or loons . . .
Here comes the snow, that ought to make the children
happy as parrots flying over a gorge with a bamboo bridge
built like a xylophone and fruit bats hanging upside down
who look at the world and decide to go airy in ardent pursuit
of a plum. But what does the inner world know
of the outer? And will I find out soon? That word,
that word has kept me company all my life.

Perpetually
Attempting to Soar

A boy from Brooklyn used to cruise on summer nights.
As soon as he'd hit sixty he'd hold his hand out the window,
cupping it around the wind. He'd been assured
this is exactly how a woman's breast feels when you put
your hand around it and apply a little pressure. Now he knew,
and he loved it. Night after night, again and again, until
the weather grew cold and he had to roll the window up.
For many years afterwards he was perpetually attempting
to soar. One winter's night, holding his wife's breast
in his hand, he closed his eyes and wanted to weep.
He loved her, but it was the wind he imagined now.
As he grew older, he loved the word *etcetera* and refused
to abbreviate it. He loved sweet white butter. He often
pretended to be playing the organ. On one of his last mornings,
he noticed the shape of his face molded in the pillow.
He shook it out, but the next morning it reappeared.

Talking to Strangers

Do you see sunspots? A strong, terrible love where
there isn't any? A demoiselle crane talking to a lama
duck? Very interesting, but there's nothing in it.
Some people take electric roses and plant them in a field
to bring the field down to earth.
There's nothing wrong with that. Put down your book.
Look at me when I talk to you. I'm the oxygen mask
that comes dangling down in a plane.
I'm here to help you be garrulous.
I'm not interested in your family—not your mother,
father, brother, sister, son, daughter, lover or
dog. In France, they used to kill themselves if
a dinner party went wrong. That's a great idea.
Are you interested in orphan-types who turn out
to be kings, or kings who come to nothing?
What's the difference between watching and looking?
Doff your garb. I'm sorry, but the loggerhead turtles
off the Carolina coast are leaving for Africa tonight.
Would you like an ice-cold pear instead?
Walking into the store is like entering
the delicate refrain of a Christmas poem.
What more could you want? Siddhartha said
someone who brushes against you in the street
has shared an experience with you for five hundred lives.
Can bottles bobbing on the open sea
be said to move at all?

The Brooch

After Keats's death, Severn wanted to have made
a gold brooch in the shape of a lyre
with strands of John's hair for the strings.
In Oceania this doesn't amount to a thing.
The Hawaiian king stood resplendent
in his cape of feathers.
Ninety thousand birds were captured and killed
for their orange and yellow wings.
It took a century to complete, a century
for a man to become a bird.
Keats took a few minutes one afternoon
while writing a letter.
Still, there is no pin:
in all of Rome, Severn could not find a goldsmith
who could crimp the hair-strings in.

The Cart

The empty grocery cart is beginning to roll
across the empty parking lot. It's beginning to act
like Marlon Brando might if no one were watching.
It's a joyous sight, but it might not end all that
happily, the way someone light in the head
does something charming and winds up dead.
My thoughts are so heavy, you couldn't lift
the bier. They are so light and stray so far
someone in a uniform wants to bring them in.
The world might be in agony, but I don't think so.
Somewhere a woman is swathed in black veils
and smiling too. It might be the eve of her baptism,
the day after her son hit a pole.
How can she signal her acceptance of life?
What if a hummingbird enters her mouth? I hate
the thought, whizzing by in red clothes.
Yet I admire its gloves. Hands are unbearably beautiful.
They hold on to things. They let things go.

The March

The sweetpeas turn blue as they die. I guess
they sweeten while other things sour. The clock
loses fifteen minutes every two days. The long
meadow grasses are lying on their sides. To be summer
all summer long makes a body want to drop. A man
who knew John Philip Sousa said genius is making
the irrational inevitable. I'm inclined to agree.
It's irrational that the planet came to be and then
came to this: a beautiful country summer that can barely
keep its head up, coupled with long wars that turn the clouds
blue. Plus the fact we die. God was a genius. I know
I should change my life, the way grapes change to wine,
but I can't change my mind. Did you know you can make wine
out of anything? It's the color of blood before blood meets
oxygen. Here, have some. If you don't mind I'd like to put on
a military march. Look at the evening meadow! Of course,
underneath it all, the insects are tearing each other to pieces.
You know, if it's just the same with you I think I'll sit here
awhile before I turn in. Suit yourself. There's no sense
in arguing. Could we hear that again? It perks a body up.

Ancestors

The best thing that ever happened to me
was that my grandparents all died
before I was born.
I've never had a sense of who I am,
and in that regard I've been lucky.
It's only natural
I know a little about them.
One grandfather worked a steel lathe,
cut off his finger and opened a bar.
The other one went to school, became
a pharmacist and owned a marvelously
tidy drugstore. It had a soda fountain
and in the only photograph I have
he's standing behind the Moxie tap
wearing a white paper hat.
One of my grandmothers, who outlived them all,
died of either a broken heart or diabetes.
The other grandmother was sadly senile
and died peacefully in her sleep.
I have a mania for soap and cologne,
hairpins and talc, but so do many of my friends
who never had a pharmacy in their past.
With the extent of my knowledge I've done okay.
I won a cakewalk once, and another time—

[handwritten margin notes:] prose, plain, but always with a pendulum weight of movement — our line revealing, opening by next.

at a seaside carnival—a painted plate
in the shape of Rhode Island.
I don't need a quietus to sleep.
I don't need an alarm to wake.
All dreams have tragic implications.
I have the same one every year:
in Sarajevo, a queue of men
line up to have their fezzes ironed.

The Butcher's Story

When I was a boy
a young man from our village
was missing for three days.
My father, my uncle and I
went looking for him in a cart
drawn by our horse, Samuel.
We went deep into the swamp
where we found three petrified trees,
gigantic and glorious. From them
we make beautiful cabinets,
polished like glass.

A poem need
can lightness, too

It's enough for a
make something
wondrous to
look
at.

The Hand

The teacher asks a question.
You know the answer, you suspect
you are the only one in the classroom
who knows the answer, because the person
in question is yourself, and on that
you are the greatest living authority,
but you don't raise your hand.
You raise the top of your desk
and take out an apple.
You look out the window.
You don't raise your hand and there is
some essential beauty in your fingers,
which aren't even drumming, but lie
flat and peaceful.
The teacher repeats the question.
Outside the window, on an overhanging branch,
a robin is ruffling its feathers
and spring is in the air.

Minor Figure

At one point, you have to sift the sand to even glimpse
the eroded smile of God's exhaustion. And He is exhausted.
He's been playing Ozymandias backwards and forwards.
He loves to watch the sand leap up and form a throne. He loves
to watch it fall. He loves the archaeologist, unearthing his first
bone. He loves Nebraska, where the wheat plays *boules* with itself,
and the memory of Poulenc's ocelot walking in the *bois*, the sky
after sunset strangely blue. A Dutch landscape painted in Italy
is especially exhausting, as is anything intensely observed
in the dark: fungi, wild cabbage, the rotting stumps of birch.
All the immaterial factors: some matches, a bent spoon and
broken button asleep in the ditch. A couple of coins in the drawer
back at the motel. They belong to the archaeologist who will never
claim them, who has lost as many pennies as there were concubines
in the Byzantine harem. Should a portion of God's earnest work
be wasted? Colonel Mustard in the conservatory with a candlestick.
He loves all these things equally, with the same amount of
exasperation and regard you might have for a statue, or the desert,
or the moths that sometimes settle in bags of flour, surprising you
when you open the flap and some of the flour appears to escape.
He no longer knows what is divine and what is human, and His
favorite example is how Adam Pynacker, a nobody, just last November
stood in his Andean castle near an open window and watched
a piece of cloud break off and wander into the little room.

Glory

The autumn aster, those lavender ones,
and the dark-blooming sedum
are beginning to bloom in the rainy earth
with the remote intensity of a dream. These things
take over. I am a glorifier, not very high up
on the vocational chart, and I glorify everything I see,
everything I can think of. I want ordinary men and women,
brushing their teeth, to feel the ocean in their mouth.
I am going to glorify the sink with toothpaste spat in it.
I am going to say it's a stretch of beach where the foam
rolls back and leaves little shells. Ordinary people
with a fear of worldly things, illness, pain, accidents,
poverty, of dark, of being alone, of misfortune.
The fears of everyday life. People who quietly and secretly
bear their dread, who do not speak freely of it to others.
People who have difficulty separating themselves
from the world around them, like a spider hanging
off the spike of a spider mum, in an inland autumn,
away from the sea, away from that most unfortunate nation
where people are butterballs dying of meat and drink.
I want to glorify the even tinier spiders in the belly of the spider
and in the closed knot of the mum's corolla, so this is likely
to go on into winter. Didn't I say we were speaking of autumn
with the remote intensity of a dream? The deckle edge of a cloud:

blood seeping through a bandage. Three bleached beech leaves
hanging on a twig. A pair of ruined mushrooms. The incumbent
snow. The very air. The imported light. All autumn struggling
to be gay, as people do in the midst of their woe.
I met a psychic who told me my position in the universe
but could not find the candy she hid from her grandkids.
The ordinary fear of losing one's mind. You rinse the sink,
walk out into the October sunshine, and look for it
by beginning to think. That's when I saw the autumn aster,
the sedum blooming in a purple field. The psychic said
I must see the word *glory* emblazoned on my chest. Secretly
I was hoping for a better word. I would have chosen for myself
an ordinary one like *orchid* or *paw*.
Something that would have no meaning in the astral realm.
One doesn't want to glorify everything. What might I *actually say*
when confronted with the view from K2? I'm not sure
I would say anything. What's your opinion?
You're a man with a corona in your mouth,
a woman with a cottonball in her purse,
what's your conception of the world?

The Wild Rose Bush

Undone chore: pruning the wild rose bush. If
I had pruned the wild rose bush today, my life
could continue walking on new stilts, I would have
a better view of the future and be able to go further
than I can imagine at this moment. But the bush
has been pruned many times already, it has lived through
sixty years of childhood, it has felt its hips swell
and offered their red pips to the birds, it has watched
the bee pumping the foxglove, swelling her cups
with astonishing quickness, and heard the enormous roses
applauding, it has died of embarrassment and never been able
to do a thing about it, the way I can't bring myself to do
a simple chore like pruning, which is good for the world,
which pulls the world back from the brink of disaster,
which helps it forget its recent grief and not so recent grief
and ancient grief. You can hardly call me human,
though I own a pair of clippers. I have never suffered
and I have never known a hero. My father never said or did
anything of interest. He never said "If you are angry
pour everything you have ever eaten into the sea,
let the sea foam at the mouth, keep your own lips clean."
He never said that. He just sat in a comfortable chair
and let the news slip out of his hands and onto the floor.
He could not compete with it. He didn't even try. He seemed

to reach a point where he realized the news would go on without him, long after his little nap, and later his death. When he reached that point his head lolled to one side, the way a rose will if left unwatered.

Sometimes I say he was saved.

The Balloon

Rain scanty, fodder scarce. Or the children's feet
are muddy. There's no bread. A sheep ate the heart
of Thomas Hardy, so that another sheep's heart
had to do in the terrible pinch and be laid to rest
next to the novelist's wife. Have you ever seen
a sock stiffening with real blood, as if it had
a sweet red voice like the hard-to-speak-to toys
we had a heart-to-heart with when we were ten?
Some persons are picking through the rubble.
Someone's found a colander and is sifting
for his other shoe, some coins, his daughter, her bear,
the bear's undazzled eye—
which he finds and sews on his coat
and only then can the bear see the man for what he is,
an animal that needs to be talked to.
At this time a black balloon rises over the municipal
ruins, and no one knows what it means.

Perfect Reader

I spend all day in my office, reading a poem
by Stevens, pretending I wrote it myself,
which is what happens when someone is lonely
and decides to go shopping and meets another customer
and they buy the same thing. But I come to my senses,
and decide when Stevens wrote the poem he was *thinking*
of me, the way all my old lovers think of me
whenever they lift their kids or carry the trash,
and standing outside the store I think of them:
I throw my arms around a tree, I kiss the pink
and peeling bark, its dead skin, and the papery
feel of its fucked-up beauty arouses me, lends my life
a certain gait, like the stout man walking to work
who sees a peony in his neighbor's yard and thinks *ah,
there is a subject of white interpolation*, and then
the petals fall apart for a long time, as long as it takes
summer to turn to snow, and I go home at the end and watch
the news about the homeless couple who met in the park,
and then the weather, to see how they will feel tomorrow.

Tilapia

I walk into the restaurant, a genetic legacy.
I feel like eating a little fish fried to death
with a sprig of parsley over one eye.
You have to engage your dinner in its own mortality!
At the same time you must order what you want.
This fish (Ti LAH pee ah), from humble origins along
the Nile, is popular in Israel but did not vault to stardom
until raised in earnest by Costa Ricans.
From exposure you will gain success or die.
Christ did both and this is the fish (my waiter's word)
that He multiplied and thrust upon the multitudes.
A miracle that it should lie before me! A miracle
that if I remove the silver backing—courage!—
I am invited to partake of its tender core. And thus
tenderly do I love thee, little fish, even as I suffer
the death of my mother and the death of my father
and the death of all our days. I will rinse my mouth.
I will rise from this table and read meaning into the sea.
I will depart through that revolving door, which knows
no beginning and has no end, and upon my reentry
into the burning thoroughfare, I will thread my way
through the crowds, I will come upon a humble fruit stand,
where in your name and the name of thousands just like you,
I will ask for a lemon. This act, ounce for ounce, if executed
in perfect faith, will rip the cellophane off the world.

The Passing of Time

My mother has been dead six months
when my father remembers, as if for
the first time, that she is dead
and pads out across his deck
to lower the flag to half-mast.
Seeing that it already hangs midway
on the pole (snapping at the wind,
collapsed in damp heat, as if it were
her hair) he is startled and asks
Who died? I say Mother and after a while
he says Ah! then let it fly a little longer.

When Adults Talk

I am not even vaguely interested,
though for a quarter I could be.

I was not allowed to move but when my leg went dead
I cheered it on to first place.

When they whisper they ought to wear a lead vest.
Their lips look like personified oysters.

When they shout it is usually addressed
to the dead body who owned this body before us.

We can safely assume one of them is born
every minute of the day.

When my rabbit ran away it was a great relief.
I could not say so—who would understand?—

So I cried for a week.

Marked

Because I was not marked.
Because I had neither fame
nor beauty nor inquisitiveness.
Because I did not ask.
Because I used my hands.
Because I ate potatoes in dirty jackets
fished from the rocks.
Because I used a pail at night.
Because when Betty C. explained
to Betty D. the nature of the problem
I did not understand.
Because I had no silver.
Because I was like my mother before me
and kept to myself mostly.
Because humanity used the footpath.
Because my backbone started to rot.
Because I finished my term on earth
and had no knowledge of either
fear nor care, no morning knowledge,
no knowledge of evening,
and those who came before
and those following after
had no more knowledge of me
than I had of them.

Argosy

I was born with a jug on my head.
Oregano grew wild on the craggy island,
and in caves honey could be gathered
with a slotted branch. I was his housekeeper.
As he was a priest, I had to be over fifty:
I was not, but I looked it. I chopped mushrooms
the size of his foot. One evening my hand
was on the knife. He put his hand on mine.
Be careful, he said, when you make offerings
to the gods. Months later, I gave birth.
The baby's screams were berserk, like a bird over
the ocean, but she grew strong and wed and left.
He found her again and they had a son together.
A few millennia later, I was in bed but couldn't
sleep, I walked to the bathroom for a glass of water
and realized from this journey on I would drink alone,
that all the public fountains had been condemned,
crumbled, passed out of fashion forever.
I looked around: a rack of toothbrushes stood out
like stone maidens no longer supporting a roof.
The rubber picks on their bases gave me the strength
normally associated with spears.

Sentimental Education

Ann Galbraith
loves Barry Soyers.

Please pray for Lucius Fenn
who suffers greatly whilst shaking hands.

Bonny Polton
loves a pug named Cowl.

Please pray for Olina Korsk
who holds the record for missing fingers.

Leon Bendrix loves Odelia Jonson
who loves Kurt who loves Carlos who loves Paul.

Please pray for Cortland Filby
who handles a dead wasp, a conceit for his mother.

Harold loves looking at Londa's hair under the microscope.
Londa loves plaiting the mane of her pony.

Please pray for Fancy Dancer
who is troubled by the vibrissa in his nostrils.

Nadine St. Clair loves Ogden Smythe
who loves blowing his nose on postage stamps.

Please pray for William Shakespeare
who does not know how much we love him, miss him, and think of him.

Yukiko Pearl loves the little bits of toffee
that fall to the floor when Jeffrey is done with his snack.

Please pray for the florist Marieko
who wraps roses in a paper cone then punches the wrong code.

Muriel Frame loves retelling the incident
that happened on the afternoon of November third.

Please pray for our teacher Ursula Twombly
who does not know the half of it.

By the radiator in a wooden chair
wearing woolen stockings sits a little girl
in a dunce's cap, a paper cone rolled to a point
and inverted on her hair; she's got her hands
in her lap and her head bowed down, her chin
is trembling with having been singled out like this
and she is sincere in her fervent wish to die.

Take it away and give it to the Tartars
who roll gloriously into battle.

Chilly Autumn Evenings

On chilly autumn evenings I build a bonfire
and think of the woodchuck, a waddling rodent
who can no longer fit in any of the tunnels
he's built, their labyrinth a sorrow
to his forlorn highness who has one eye,
even it nearly buried in old hair.
What does place mean to him?
A chunk of land thrown out
with the rest. A bigger chunk
on which he sits and thinks.
How inaccurate of me, but moths
are too great a subject for one lifetime.
Winter passes, a powdery flounce.
The stars oscillate in their panic.
On brisk spring nights
I can hear the frogs singing in their disbelief.
What has happened to the woodchuck?
Summer goes about her work evenly, and soon
the cold will force a shaft from the moon
to the bonfire, an enormous eyebeam
from which, my friends,
we need to hide.

The Jewel

Night, and the coffers are empty.
An emerald in a truck rumbles away
to the other side of the earth.
A little girl with her pail and shovel packs up
while corpses revolve in the sea,
no more than a cavalry of undulation.
Quite the bedtime story. Papa, what happens next?
Nothing much. We go to sleep,
the jewel comes back and all is well.
The little girl gets sandy building herself a home.
The corpses are clean as diamonds in a museum,
the kind that turn when you press a button
and an eerie green light shines down on them.
And when I sleep you peep in on me?
Yes, and you are safe as baggage in the hold
beneath a bus, and not one passenger knows
the lovely thing that shifts below
or cares what happens next.

County Fair

Mrs. Oakley entered the category of Other Muffin
(that being the one where blueberries were denied):
Not uniform in shape or color. Not standard!
No award. Not a difficult decision. Her doughnut
fared no better, was shriveled by noon, its shadow
in grease on the paper plate—
no one should get hurt at the county fair
but life is a laminar surface of surfaces
and though Mrs. Oakley to her continuous credit
continuously bakes in seven categories annually
from the marquee a letter occasionally falls.
In Düsseldorf a mechanic compared premium petrol
to caviar, great sex to Sacher tortes.
The philosophers concurred: these thoughts
fall apart when you think them.
Neither deserves an award.
Rise up, Mrs. Oakley, you are not alone!

The Letter

Beloved, men in thick green coats came crunching
through the snow, the insignia on their shoulders
of uncertain origin, a country I could not be sure of,
a salute so terrifying I heard myself lying to avoid
arrest, and was arrested along with Jocko, whose tear
had snapped off, a tiny icicle he put in his mouth.
We were taken to the ice prison, a palace encrusted
with hoarfrost, its dome lit from within. Jocko admired
the wiring, he kicked the walls to test the strength
of his new boots. A television stood in a block of ice,
its blue image still moving like a liquid center.
You asked for my innermost thoughts. I wonder will I
ever see a grape again? When I think of the vineyard
where we met in October—when you dropped a cluster
custom insisted you be kissed by a stranger—how after
the harvest we plunged into a stream so icy our palms
turned pink. It seemed our future was sealed. Everyone
said so. It is quiet here. Not closing our ranks
weakens us hugely. The snowflakes fall in a featureless
bath. I am the stranger who kissed you. On sunny days
each tree is a glittering chandelier. The power of
mindless beauty! Jocko told a joke and has been dead
since May. A bullethole in his forehead the officers
call a third eye. For a month I milked a barnful of

cows. It is a lot like cleansing a chandelier. Wipe
and polish, wipe and polish, round and round you go.
I have lost my spectacles. Is the book I was reading
still open by the side of our bed? Treat it as a bookmark
saving my place in our story.

(here the letter breaks off)

Pressed for Details

I was given a new pair of potholders on my birthday.
I smelled lime blossoms for the first time. I discovered
the stories of Robert Walser and so you could say
I fell in love with a dead man. My mother died
and in this fulfilled my lifelong wish to put bluebonnets
on a grave. My father lost his memory and so became
what he had always been—a simple man. I learned everything
about the former Soviet Union, but if pressed for details
I'd fail you. One morning—just like that—someone called
seagulls *rats with wings*. I saw a young lady—a girl really—
sitting on the beach in a red bathing suit, sobbing.
The front of her suit was soaked. All around her
the seagulls lowered themselves like helicopters.
Miss Manners of the *Daily News* says if you cannot offer
concrete help, it is best to say nothing. What are you going to do
to alleviate the problem? Give her a job? Offer her your heart?
What you are contemplating is simply saying you are sorry
as you go on your own way. This notifies the lady she is a spectacle,
causing more discomfort. Therefore Miss Manners invokes the rule
for physical accident: don't stand and gawk. Don't be a seagull.
Seagulls get shot at the end of great plays.
I carry this advice with me into the next year. You could say
I walk away from it and toward it at the same time.
Not getting any younger, whom have I helped? Heavenly lime blossoms!
Most respectful sir: Walser wrote this curious form of address
brings the assurance the writer confronts you quite coldly.

The Edge

This is the story of why my shoes
lie in a row at the bottom of my closet.
In the state of Virginia, on the North American
continent, there was a wasp.
Perhaps it was a yellow jacket, I'm not sure,
and though I care very deeply and desire to be
as refined as possible, this is also a story
of resignation. Was it there I read Wordsworth?
I don't remember, but one summer vacation
I began to notice little things in nature,
like the wild azalea, its salmon pinkening
to a crustacean rose, each bloom a tiny head
with mouth and horns, and when I looked closely
I saw a spider skitter between blooms,
I saw a long spindle of drool, I saw a single globe
of some kind of moisture, as if earth's image
were fastened to the end of a stick.
This kind of thinking led to a palace, the defining
carpet unrolled, and I entered the spiritual Versailles
of wannabes on tiny misshapen heels.
How close I came to meeting the king
I'll never know, I only know I approached him
(on tiny misshapen heels)
before the wasp, whatever, fuck it, inserted himself
and sat down, plump in his gorgeous robes, on the throne
of my ivory feet. I stopped breathing then,

but took it as a sign someone was announcing my name,
that I was leaving one chamber and entering another
but did not know I would fall unfocused and alone,
half-dead on the dirty path.
For a moment—one delirious moment that curiously
marked both my rise and fall—I thought
I heard the nearby brook *singing*,
but I think now it was strangling some branch.
Later, lying on flowered sheets in the motor home,
my mother ecstatic to have me back, I could hear
the medics up front swiveling in the driver's seat,
one saying to the other *it's my dream to have me
one of these babies someday.* What a nice thing
to say, I thought. Someone brought me a donut.
So Wordsworth, crossing the Alps, lost his guide
in the mist, walked on, and later reconnoitered
with his friends. *When are we coming to the summit?*
he asked. *You've already crossed* cried the guide,
then he took his pointed stick and stuck it
in the mist. That was all a long time ago
and every morning I get up, my refinement in decline.
My shoes are stepping-stones. Much clear water
running fiercely through my closet. Afraid to cross,
slip on moss, that kind of thing. Some of my friends
ask me for details, but I just stand there
in my bare feet, terrified to look down.

Furtherness

An oak coffin covered with vines
carried on moss in a farm cart

A dusty coffin in a yellow wagon
with bright red wheels going down
the painted road

A glass coffin stifled by roses

Raining, and in the film version
an unknown god stood at a distance
watching, got in his car and left

The little black urn before
a spray of orchids in the alcove

They laid a bunch of violets at her throat
closed the white coffin
carried it out the rear door
through buttercups down to the grave

The musicians are drunk and play
loudly, stumbling down the street

Six men with sore arms

The family in a rowboat:
the coffin inhabiting the mind

Or ashes streaming like a scarf from the convertible

Or, the chorus breaks out in excelsis

Or, the soloist sang like a dilated eye

Stunning din of a sob

Salt pork on a wound

Is it ordure to speak of the widow's grief?

Who drags herself back
through a field so thick with vetch
it gives a purple tint over two or three acres
You could run through them for hours
but one thing is certain from her face
she does not want you to

Furthermore, there are pies on the table waiting

Thistle

We traveled to Palestine last Easter
to see the site of the betrayal of Christ
and saw two men in a brick enclosure
staring at a drain in the ground.
A ruthless thistle grew out of a crumbly spot
in the wall. We traveled to Chile to experience
the driest spot on earth, at a roadside shrine
the Virgin had a long eyelash on her lips
and a ruthless thistle growing
out of a crumbly spot on her side.
We traveled to Brazil to see Pelé in action
but the papers announced he had stepped on a thistle.
How did the Japanese princess know it was her hairpin
found in a subway station? In Provence
there is an old tree famous for its bark,
packed with fading pigments:
someone scraped a palette there. Saw that,
stopped in a shop run by Scots and bought
a teapot with a thistle on top.
O ruthless thistle, match in the dark,
you can talk to anyone about the weather
but only to your closest friends
can you mention the light.

Nothing Like the Earth

If it is winter in the book

spring surprises me   when I look up   and though I know

there is nothing like the earth   though I know

the lilies in the yard   throw open the doors of the heart

with wondrous force   and I am a buck-merino   a dandy little

buck-merino   jumping with felicity over the fence

and I shall not want   He maketh me lie down on the bed

to read   so I do not know which is the ephemera

the lilies   or the boy in winter whose fate is at a toss

Can anything save the appalling youth brightened with

intense pulse or that deep & wailing cry allotted to his crow?

Yea, though I walk through the valley of these things

there is a rich fever   that never foams

a swatch of fastidious root fastened to a rock

like a hand gripping a doorknob   unable to move

a tentacle of intent that may yet restore

the song of the lute to the lily   or the glory of the crow

to the boy

Full Moon

The white spot to the upper left
which looks like the pith plug
in a peeled orange is the crater Tycho.
I have never been there. Perhaps one day
you will. I saw many jackets in the coatroom
but none of them were his. I know someone
who is alive somewhere.
It is embarrassing to be alive.
Sometimes you have to stand out on the street
and look upwards, and then you have to pretend
the stone at your feet
is not an object of observation,
when it is.

Silk Land

Nothing's happened, there are no examples.
At most I feel an exceptionally light bug
has been bothering me.
It's dead on the maternity ward
and I've never even *seen* bougainvillea
so this gardening rag is a bust.
There's a rustle of forms.
Aline comes in at midnight
and gives me a penny for my thoughts.
She's like a mid-Atlantic Coke machine
that's out of order. Bob comes in at six
and tells me about the weekend.
He screwed behind sandbags, lurched
down the beach, blacked out
but didn't drown.
I crawl straight back to the depths of
my mother's drawer, sunk among the lingerie.

Against the Sky

The stamens of the lily stiffen into claws.
Gentle lily!
The lily begins to eat us all.
When two angels met in a closed room
was there not a lily on the table between them
and did not the lily on the table between them
have a hunger sent from God?
Don't ask me that. I no longer have a heart
that can describe the world.
Don't ask me that, or I shall needlepoint
my own head.
We who are about to die cannot know such things.
This is not where we know such things.
We lean against the sky,
and beyond that—
the dark origin of all this nonsense
where words stray and are not recovered.
Even if you push embers into their apertures.
Don't ask me that. Even if the changeling
tries to consume me, and spits me out
in a sparked shower.

Mariposa and the Doll

I perceive nothing but the wild, wild sob of agony.
We must look into this, Posey, said her father.
Too many pretty dolls might compose the problem.

                              Then he took
an old tongueless boot and turned it upside down,
and on the flat horseshoe of its decomposed heel
he hammered three nails: two for the eyes and one
for the nose. Then he took a rag that had become a rag
and tied it round the throat. He sat the shoedoll on her lap
and left. Mariposa sat with the doll and waited but
nothing happened between them. She threw the shoe off—
I've no one to talk to!—when the doll stirred, sighing,
and said   The lurid light of a May morning and the hills
a cast of purplish beans on the horizon, and the violent freshness
of our awakening, like a plow turning the black earth,
and still the deeper-than-you-can-furrow feeling that today
is but a placebo for tomorrow: such is the volatile fact
of our hidden inertia.

Thereafter the long afternoons were much shortened.

Patina

In the village of Akishino,
a woman pounding cloth with a stone
on a stone until sunlight turns to dusk.
Autumn deepening all around.
When will the cloth be ready?
In two, in three hundred years
it becomes a scroll hanging in a museum
and the guard turns to look at it every night
before turning off the lights. He turns to look at it
because he does not like it, it glows,
and he is a suspicious man,
well suited to his job.
At home before going to bed
he looks at his wife for a long time
as though she were a secret.
Although far from young
her skin is beautiful when it sleeps.
He turns the lamp off.
Everything is serious in the dark.
He thinks in the morning he will ask her
to wash the sheets more often. Or
less frequently, he can't decide.

Mercy

God have mercy on me. This is the diary of a lost soul
(I am also the author of *No Bed of Roses*). Apparently
I cannot live without parentheses. To live without
parentheses would be as scary as living without
parents, I mean, to have been born out of nothing.
When someone stands before you and puts their hands
on your hips they are acting like parentheses,
which is why a great many thinkers come from Paris,
where lovers embrace on the quays and intellectuals
watch them from windows, taking notes. I will buy anything
that comes from Paris, which is another reason God
should have mercy on me. I believe Paris is a place where
everyone is marvelously alive, each in their own way,
and the moon is different, too—it never disappears or goes
away, it never looks like a parenthesis, but grows continually
round till it breaks of its own weight and pieces of it fall
like fireworks (!) and the lovers watch and the intellectuals
take notes and everything is endlessly fascinating
in a spectacular way. I should be more Parisian. That is
my thesis. But I know from the movies Paris is nothing
like that, it is full of motorcycles and crooks and the clothing
is all too small because no one cares enough to replace it
and people continually grow out of it without even bothering

to notice. But I notice. From my little apartment in Massachusetts
I notice and I care. God have mercy on me!
I would lie down and put a dagger in my heart
if I only knew how and where and why.

Among the Musk Ox People

They were aesthetes, which means
I was forced to eat a hard peach,
commissioned to paint a twelve-foot abstraction
based on watching host cells collaborate
in bacterial infection, and at night
chewed the soles of their mukluks
till they were soft again.
If I ventured outside the igloo
and saw a celebrity,
I felt so inferior
I wanted to die.
To conceal my envy
I was given dark glasses.
If, on the other hand, I encountered
someone to whom I was vastly superior,
one of those ill-clad, raving, wandering hags,
I felt ashamed and wanted to die.
To appease my guilt
they were given by the Elders a little of my grub.
If I met with an Ordinary,
someone not dissimilar to myself,
with dissatisfactions roughly the same,
I felt the world was senseless
supporting so many look-alikes

and again I asked to die:
life reached a maddening peak
out there on the ice when
we were hunting and could move only our eyes.
Still, like a seal reaching his blowhole
in the dark, every seventy-two hours
I came to my senses for thirteen minutes
and continued to live with the knowledge
that deep in the oyster bed of my blood
layered spheres continued to build round
my name, cold, calciferous, and forgotten.
When The Giant Orphan At The Bottom Of The Sea
appeared in my dreams,
demanding I write the story
of three generations of Ox women
resulting in the birth of a performance artist,
I knew I would need a knife, gun, needles,
kettle, scissors, and soap,
and gave up, at last, my finest skins.
I made my escape across the shrouded inlet
away from those who believe that outside
our minds there is only mist,
and with my skills at flensing
never feared for the future.

Seven Postcards from Dover

I

The teacher said *inner truth*
and the chalk said *like a fresco inside the earth*
that no one has ever seen
and one day decides to be discovered
and begins to breathe—
do you know what that means?

II

The child broke the chalk.
The mother said *be strong*.
The child said *when I die I want to be a dwarf.*

III

A detective has just drawn a circle
with a piece of chalk, a private circle
from which the victim will eventually look
up, not at random, not at will,
but when it calls to her,
the chalk, the crushed bones

of sea creatures who ringed the earth
when it was underwater.

IV

A man sits in the bathhouse
in a deep tub
of fizzling yellow water
that surrounds every hair on his body
and makes it stand upright.
When the attendant comes, she will
clean the tub by moving her hand
slowly around the ring, like a snail.

V

An atoll is a ring of coral
protecting a tureen of plankton.
It is easy and Japanese to be sad
knowing something is going to pass.
He put the ring on her chalky finger.

VI

Long after chalk had passed out of use,
carpenters still felt for it in their pockets
and looked aimlessly at the sky.

VII

The cathedral was roofless.
It began to snow inside.
A half-broken pillar in the nave
grew taller.

The Tragic Drama of Joy

Late that night it rained so hard the world
    seemed flattened for good.
But the grocer knew the earth had a big gut
    and could hold more than enough.
When he went out to receive a shipment of cat food
    the stays of his umbrella were bent.
It took some time to fix them and when he got to his shop
    the truck had already left.
On a whim he went inside and brought home
    a bottle of wine for his wife.
Have you gone crazy? she said. They didn't uncork it,
    but he felt something nonetheless.
That wonderful click his umbrella had made
    when it finally opened for good!

The Great Loneliness

By March the hay bales were ripped open

exposed in the fields

like bloated gray mice

who died in December.

I came upon them at dusk

and their attar lifted my spine

until I felt like turning over an old leaf.

So I walked on, a walking pitchfork.

From every maple hung a bucket or two

collecting blood to be distributed across America

so people could rise from their breakfast

healthy, hoping to make a go of it again.

Now this is a riddled explanation

but I am a historian of pagan means

and must walk five miles a day

to cover the period I will call

The Great Loneliness

and the name will stick so successfully

that for years afterwards children will complain

at meals and on sunny days and in the autumn and at Easter

that their parents are unnecessarily mute

and their parents will look down harshly

upon the plates and beach towels and leaves and bunnies

and say *you don't know what you are talking about*

you never lived through The Great Loneliness
and if you had you would never speak.
And the children will turn away
and consider the words, or lack of them,
and how one possible explanation
might be that inside our bodies
skeletons grow at an increasingly secretive rate,
though they never mention it,
even amongst themselves.

The Feast

I have a goblet. I will share it with you.

Here is a table. The goblet is on it.

There is a goose. We will cook it with our breath—done—

and set it on the table. Now we have a goblet and a goose.

All we need are candles and some wine, some bread.

Everything we need is now upon the table.

Let us eat the goose. It is good to eat the goose,

we want it to be gone. We want the goose inside ourselves.

What lovely feelings all around! They are in the goblet

and in our eyeballs and in the flickering flames.

May I put the candle in your mouth? Let us eat the table.

Let us break its legs and turn it upside down.

Let us tear the bread and stuff it inside the goose

inside ourselves. Let the lovely feelings go the way of flesh.

Put the eyeballs in the goblet and flambé them there.

Some winters are harder than others.

Let us burn it all and eat it all.

Everything is on its knees.

Now there is nothing left,

and I will not share it with anyone.

Zettel

A piece of paper fell out of the book
and drifted to the floor.
It was the first time I had witnessed
a birth, and I was shocked.
What a magnificent cause.
My entire brain plunged into thoughts
connected with the tiny object.
Do people become people for different reasons?
Ever yours. Evermore the imperial tether of
adult tenderness, the full radius of listening
at night, paired with horses grazing on ice:
out of my eye's corner I will never lose you,
the way a snow flea jumps on snow, following
one hoof, one print, one word, one minute
to the next. You need never know.
It was very quiet then for a long time,
after I bent down and picked it up.

Japanese Bloodgod

I feed my sorrow

I feed my sorrow spinach

I feed my sorrow eggs

I feed my sorrow sunflowers

I feed my sorrow pineapples and newspapers and trash

There is a cake rising for my sorrow

I feed it opium and I buy Scotch tape for it

I buy batteries for my sorrow

I throw coins at my sorrow

I look at it through binoculars

I throw lavender on the sheets of my sorrow

I burn frankincense for my sorrow

I starch my sorrow

I iron it flat, then I fold it again

I buy blueberries for my sorrow

Like all things, it likes itself

It likes what it is made of

When I want to touch it

I fill the sink with hot water

and add a submarine

Magnificat

O Lord, I did walk upon the earth
and my footprints did keep pace with the rain
and I did note, I did note where orange birds
flew up from the puddles thou hast made
and where the toads leapt from your trenches,
but nowhere was there that I could go
for I could not rise from the firmament
upon which I was placed, and nowhere could I
so I kept until I could no more straight
then bent said *I am down to make room for the more*
and you half hearing did send me down
into the soul of another by mistakes
and I would like to thank you for it
from where I lie, risen in the eye of the other.

My Life as a Farmer

BY JAMES DEAN

Being a farmer is the loneliest thing in the world.
The field is like a religion you dedicate yourself
to, and when there's a cloudburst you can't be
elsewhere. Hopefulness and a worrisome nature
are among the attributes of a basically farming man.
You're all alone with your seeds and your concentration.
You don't have time to see friends and it's not for them
to understand. You don't have anybody, only a pig
and some chickens, and you have to think for them.
You're all alone with their feed and your concentration
and that's all you have. You're a farmer.

Critique of Little Errors

I was a failure as a gingerbread baker,
I was a failure at drawing grasshoppers,
a failure as a tailor, a failure
as the official keeper of tariffs on all signet rings,
and I failed to put the cap back on the glue.
But it has been a beautiful day,
go down the street as far as you can go
and ask anybody.
The serpentine hours circumvented it,
the sunset couldn't eat its edges,
eyes everywhere unfrosted.
When I am old and selling nutmegs
I will be a failure at remembering
how when the syllabub drinkers beat the barmaids
the barmaids expired in their aprons on the floor
and I prevented it from happening.
Even so, this was the one day
no one seemed to care that the cap
was making trips in the dumbwaiter.

Concerning
Essential Existence

The horse mounted the mare slowly and precisely
and then stopped.

He was profoundly disturbed by a piece of straw.

He was profoundly distracted by the sad toy
upside down in the tree.

He was profoundly disengaged by half a cloud
in the corner of his wet eye.

And then he continued.

Nothing is forgot by lovers
except who they are.

Do Not Disturb

In a milk white mist in the middle of the wood
there are two dead vowels.

The vowels in the wood are cared for by birds
who cover them in strawberry leaves

and in the winter when the bodies are mounded
with snow, owls keep a vigil
from a nearby branch
by the light of the moon.

Poor vowels in the wood!
Poor vowels in the wood!

They can't remember the vows in the wood
when they did woo.

How before they were dead
they lay on their backs
and looked at the clouds,
speaking softly to one another for hours.

The Little I Saw of Cuba

She regained her sight for five days and she said
I cannot be left alone with the lettuce
I cannot be left alone with the lettuce—
the salad strewn in the salad bowl,
the bite-sized leaves and the red shreds
terrified her with tremendous color
and then she was blind again—
operation unsuccessful—
and I remember one other thing:
she traveled.
This surprised me for I could see
and I did not travel
and the contrast terrified me
while making a kind of calm sense,
especially when I was sleeping,
for I often thought of Cuba
and felt safe in the tropics,
walking among fronds with nothing to do
but watch red lizards climbing the wall.
Of course I have never been to Cuba,
but it remains a place
where I have never found it necessary
to alter my description of anything.

In the Office of the Therapist I Behold the Extinguished Guests

The little waxed cups all crushed and the kleenex
in the basket at my feet.

Someone was here before me
drinking water and crying.

The caveman, that hairy ape,
had been drinking from the lagoon
and spat right back into it.

Sometimes the smoke from the fires
made his eyes water

and this became associated
with the sick and the dying
who were laid out by the fires
while the others went hunting.

And always upon entering the great indoors
in inclement weather, I saw a chair
that had once been a wild tree.

Because his spear was dull that day
he had to pierce the boar over and over,
fountains of blood still pumping
as he dragged the carcass back.

Passing the fat around.
Eating the feet and the knuckles.

Finally telling the ones in the sooty cave
it was time to leave the future behind.

And here were the boar's eyeballs to prove it.

The Nutshell

I lay back like a canoe
and let my long hair
dredge the water.
The bluebird was *really blue,*
its breast an apricot in the sun.

I picked up a human skull
that had suffered long enough
and with my own two hands
smashed it against a rock.

I have never been to Denmark
but once at night walking
past a barroom in Chicago
I smelled something no one should have to smell
and helped him stand
and walk upright.

And once when my face was wet
with real tears, I opened
one eye to make sure
you were watching.

As a member of the world's most
intelligent audience it's only natural

you ask questions, all of which
I answer with *that's it in a nutshell*:
you can hold it in the palm of your hand,
for it is all that is made.

Why I Am Not a Good Kisser

Because I open my mouth too wide
Trying to take in the curtains behind us
And everything outside the window
Except the little black dog
Who does not like me
So at the last moment I shut my mouth.

Because Cipriano de Rore was not thinking
When he wrote his sacred and secular motets
Or there would be only one kind
And this affects my lips in terrible ways.

Advice,
experience

Because at the last minute I see a lemon
Sitting on a gravestone and that is a thing, a thing
That would appear impossible, and the kiss
Is already concluded in its entirety.

Because I learned everything about the beautiful
In a guide to the weather by Borin Van Loon, so
The nature of lenticular clouds and anticyclones
And several other things dovetail in my mind
& at once it strikes me what quality goes to form
A Good Kisser, especially at this moment, & which you
Possess so enormously—I mean when a man is capable
Of being in uncertainties, Mysteries & doubts without me

I am dreadfully afraid he will slip away
While my kiss is trying to think what to do.

Because I think you will try to read what is written
On my tongue and this causes me to interrupt with questions:
A red frock? Red stockings? And the rooster dead?
Dead of what?

Because of that other woman inside me who knows
How the red skirt and red stockings came into my mouth
But persists with the annoying questions
Leading to her genuine ignorance.

Because just when our teeth are ready to hide
I become a quisling and forget the election results
And industrial secrets leading to the manufacture
Of woolen ice cream cones, changing the futures
Of ice worms everywhere.

Can it be that even the greatest Kisser ever arrived
At his goal without putting aside numerous objections—

Because every kiss is like throwing a pair of doll eyes
Into the air and trying to follow them with your own—

However it may be, *O for a life of Kisses*
Instead of painting volcanoes!

Even if my kiss is like a paintbrush made from hairs.
Even if my kiss is squawroot, which is a scaly herb
Of the broomrape family parasitic on oaks.
Even if a sailor went to sea in me
To see what he could see in me
And all that he could see in me
Was the bottom of the deep dark sea in me.

Even though I know nothing can be gained by running
Screaming into the night, into the night like a mouth,
Into the mouth like a velvet movie theater
With planets painted on its ceiling
Where you will find me, your pod mate,
In some kind of beautiful trouble
Over moccasin stitch #3,
Which is required for my release.

Proscenium Arch

I lived like a god.

My thin back walking out the door,
my heart of mayonnaise.

I put halos on heads
and then they cursed me.

Even the posh deserve names.

And the people who went out at sunset
waiting for fear to find them—
I left obscenities on the benches.

I made all manner of transportation
miss its destination
and the signs instructing people
not to cry—I hung them.

I passed out fliers—
ten percent off if you walk ten miles.

Finally I tried to kiss someone
and they said I was drunk.

And now the real gods have come

so I can sit down,

so I can shut up early

and later act dead.

not only living
now, what that
is like —,
but having lived —
what did I
do?
How do I remember
How do I
count on
what's
real?

Oh Myrtie

She brought the tombstone home
and stood at the kitchen sink, scrubbing it.
It was small, the size of a phone book, #17.
On the numbers *one* and *seven* she used a toothbrush.
Not me. I am the one who stood at the kitchen sink
and dropped her teeth in a glass of water.
After they fizzed for a while
everything happened as it should.
I called a friend who seemed to know my name
but his voice was far away
like in a wet field or something.
What has that woman got to do with me? I wondered.
And then I began to pray.
Please don't step on our sleeping village.
Many private conversations will be crushed.

From Here to Eternity

One day you wake up
and your life is over.
But it doesn't mean
you have to die.
It means last October was yellower
than this, and this the yellowest
anyone can remember.
It means you have produced enough tears
to fill, to one-eighth of an inch
of the top, Lake Baikal,
and now someone would like to swim.
It means what it meant
to listen to the teacher
tell the story of Dante and Beatrice
and break down crying in the middle,
because his wife was taken away by the police
last night, you so happy
to be dismissed early
you and your pals broke out
a pack of cards on the tram.
It means you are more interested
in the shadows of objects than objects
themselves, and if asked to draw anything

you would only need charcoal
to convince the world
it is waiting, in the shadows
of things, and you will wait back.

A Picture of Christ

Christ had a cripple under each arm
the way people use crutches.
He had a hard glossy thick tongue
like the leaf of a camellia
and it was hanging out.
He had his picture taken this way.
He looked beat and strangely triumphant.
After all, the sun was shining again.
But the more you looked at the picture
the more you understood
exactly what those words meant:
the sun was a siren, the shining
was its singing and its song was "again."
Again and again you looked at it
and it always looked as if it had just been taken,
as if the cripples were being paid a day's wages
for five minutes' work and the camellias
had just torn off their leaves and given them away.
And you got the feeling you too were donating your time
just looking at it when you could be doing other things.

Gathered on a Friday in the Hour of Jupiter

Some sunflowers. Arched over one another
in the big pot, like so many faces vying
for a view of the procession.
And the sea was there, though it hadn't spoken yet,
so it was hard to tell what century it was
(had Mozart been born, the Alps crossed, the heart
cut open?) or if there were any thoughts
on the cruciform and the undeniable fact
only a human being could hammer another one
to a board. Just some sunflowers in a pot,
and a crowd of townspeople walking towards
the harbor (one looked like wood
and was raised above the others)
and the sea which had never spoken and held
no information in its mud-bearing heart
though everyone was walking towards it,
gathered on a Friday in the hour of Jupiter
while the sun drank the water
with the dead quiet beauty
of ancient flyless days.

How I Became Impossible

I was born shy, congenitally unable to do anything
profitable, to see anything in color, to love plums,
with a marked aversion to traveling around the room,
which is perfectly normal in infants.
Who wrote this? were my first words.
I did not like to be torched.
More snow fell than was able to melt.
I became green-eyed and in due time traveled
to other countries where I formed opinions
on hard, cold, shiny objects and soft, warm,
nappy things. Late in life I began to develop
a passion for persimmons and was absolutely delighted
when a postcard arrived for the recently departed.
I became recalcitrant, spending more and more time
with my rowboat. All my life I thought polar bears
and penguins grew up together playing side by side
on the ice, sharing the same vista, bits of blubber
and innocent lore. One day I read a scientific journal:
there are no penguins at one pole, no bears
on the other. These two, who were so long intimates
in my mind, began to drift apart, each on his own floe,
far out into the glacial seas. I realized I was becoming
impossible, more and more impossible,
and that one day it really would be true.

The Tenor of Your Yes

If you were lonely
and you saw the earth
you'd think *here is*
the end of loneliness
and I have reached it by myself.

*end of
review*

If you were sad
and you saw the kitchen
you'd think *here is*
the end of sadness
and they have prepared it
for me.

Turner painted his own
sea monsters, but hired
someone else to do
"small animals."
Apparently he could do
a great sky, but not
rabbits.

Much like god at the end.

My Happiness

I laid my happiness in a field
My happiness lay in the field and looked up at the sky
My happiness extended the same courtesy to the clouds
My happiness in the field was visible for miles around
My happiness was visible to the hawk
My happiness was fond of the beetle beside it

A porcupine lumbered by
My happiness followed it
Perhaps because it was being followed
the porcupine "stole" my happiness
My happiness lumbered along after itself, happily
We came to a road
The porcupine went into a culvert and didn't come out
And that was the end of my happiness

The Meal That Was Always There

It was a dangerous day.
The earth was shining
and the sun drank its joy.
The little goat was chomping columbine.
All the babies smelled of sweet milk.
The old folk sold their recipes.
All the women followed them.
The men ate, pulled off their boots
and wiggled their toes.
The trout responded to the water
and the hermit found his herbs nearby.
The radiance of circles had never been
wider, more one-inside-of-the-other.
Who began to feed the goat
the pages of a book?
Who began to feed the goat
the tragedies of Shakespeare?
What would we do without them?

Kiss of the Sun

If, as they say, poetry is a sign of something
among people, then let this be prearranged now,
between us, while we are still peoples: that
at the end of time, which is also the end of poetry
(and wheat and evil and insects and love),
when the entire human race gathers in the flesh,
reconstituted down to the infant's tiniest fold
and littlest nail, I will be standing at the edge
of that fathomless crowd with an orange for you,
reconstituted down to its innermost seed protected
by white thread, in case you are thirsty, which
does not at this time seem like such a wild guess,
and though there will be no poetry between us then,
at the end of time, the geese all gone with the seas,
I hope you will take it, and remember on earth
I did not know how to touch it it was all so raw,
and if by chance there is no edge to the crowd
or anything else so that I am of it,
I will take the orange and toss it as high as I can.

Pontiac

Someone in Pontiac, Michigan
thinks I am pretty.
I say you should have seen me
when I was six months old,
my flesh the flesh of a partridge,
my legs spread by a steel bar,
my perfect feet in orthopedic shoes
bolted to the bar.
I tell him the whole twentieth century
was basically a mistake.
I tell this not to him but to my bathrobe,
who is linted and old and ignores me.
She's been on dope for years.
She's never been outside.
She looks at me through the wrong end
of a telescope and goes on chewing her sleeves.
Finally I start to get dressed
and when she's lying on the bed she says
your capacity for suffering is infinite—
how much fun we could have had if it was not—
I pick her up,
and we pass the afternoon in communal affection
without which the most benign of god's creatures
would inconsolably wither.

My Timid Eternity

I am thinking how lonesome it will be in Heaven
with only George Washington and me there.
I suppose we will recite the Beatitudes
and wonder when they are coming—
the meek, the merciful, the peacemakers,
those who are pure in heart.
Roasting marshmallows in the evening
I will broach the subject of lies.
He will hand me a wig
and some leeches, which I will decline,
still thinking about the others—
if they went to the Babies Camp by mistake
we could maybe get a letter out.
Heaven should not be full of worry
but if anyone knows more about it than this,
if you have your own version—
leafy, airy, full, fountainous—
bless you, you are more lonesome
than either the General or I.

Sweet Morning

They lined up all the Psalms,
all one hundred and fifty of them,
and shot them one by one.

They threw them in a trench
made for the purpose of burying Psalms.

And did the Psalms rise up,
did they rise up singing?

Did the Psalms stay together,
did the Psalms disperse?

Did the Twenty-third Psalm escape,
and come to your house
and ask for a ride?

Imagine you are the belated passenger.
Tell what happened to you and what you saw.

I saw one hundred and fifty bathers
come to a wide, calm lake
at the end of a long, hot day.

I saw one hundred and fifty bathers
take off their clothes and swim slowly
to the other side, with a long cool joy
like that of swans and dogs.

How do you explain this?

By way of the oft-repeated.
By way of sorrow's root.
By way of the swinging lantern.
And by the faces of stars
drowned in the morning light.

The Imperial Ambassador of the Infinite

One August afternoon
he came back, after thirty years,
and they stood in the garden briefly,
no more than twenty minutes.
We know she shaded her eyes
with her hand, because someone saw her.
He held his hat in his.
We know not what they said
and I never think of it, except
when I see the windshield of a car
smashed in the street, its silver
loosed like the sea itself.
Except when I run away from home
by hiding under the bed.
Except when I think being alone
hasn't been invented yet,
except for the mirror,
and there there are two too,
standing cold and damaged and drenched
in their own awkwardness,
which is the awkwardness of Mercury

bringing a message to himself
(after so many years!), and except
when I see the bee,
stoned out of his mind,
leaving the flower forever.

After a Rain

They noticed, you see, that I was a noticing
kind of person, and so they left the dictionary
out in the rain and I noticed it,
I noticed it was open to the *rain* page,
much harm had come to it, it had aged to the age
of ninety-five paper years and I noticed *rainbow*
follows *rain* in the book, just as it does on
earth, and I noticed it was silly of me to
notice so much but I noticed there is no stationery
in heaven, I noticed an infant will grip your hand like
there is no tomorrow, while the very aged
will give you a weightless hand for the same reason,
I noticed in a loving frenzy that some are hemlocked
and others are not (believe me yours unspeakably obliged),
I noticed whoever I met in my search for entrance
into this world went too far (but that was their
destination) and I noticed the road followed roughly
the route of a zipper around a closed case,
I noticed the sea was human but no one believed me,
and that some birds have the wingspan of an inch
and some flowers the petal span of a foot yet the two
are very well suited to each other, I noticed that.
There are eight major emotional states but I forget
seven of them, I can hear the ambulance singing

but I do not think it will stop for me,
because I noticed the space between the waterfall and
the rock and I am safe there, resting in
the cradle of all there is, the way a sea horse
(when it is tired) will tie its tail to a seaweed
and rest, and there has not been, in my opinion,
enough astonishment over this fact, so now I will
withdraw my interest in the whole external world
while I am in the noticing mode, notice how I
talk to you just as if you were sitting in my lap
and not as if it were raining, not as if there were
a sheet of water between us or anything else.

Thirteen

I was thirteen,
my whole leg in a cast.
It was like lugging
a piece of pottery around.
And every human face I knew
took a pen and wrote on me.
I used to lie in bed at night
and read it.
And when I healed
they broke it—
I walked away
without a shard.
Paula? Carl? Whoever you are,
I will not be there to drink the water
beside your bed.
I read three thousand books,
and then I died.

Lines Written on
a Blank Space

I lifted the sponge
and touched the soap—
would it be gone by September?
It had been my closest companion,
it knew me well, and I felt about it
the same, though we never spoke
and I did not know where it came from
before I found it, all the while I was walking
it sat in the dark room where white light
came in through the lace curtains,
and when I came back from my walk
with the smell of wet, chopped wood
being dragged over pine needles
clinging to my clothes, my hair,
it was there, only smaller,
imperceptibly smaller, which is
the way it was made to grow—
by getting smaller—
and if this be the point
where soap begins, how
can I say it will not keep growing

after it goes away?
I lifted the soap,
I lifted my long terrible arm
and turned on the water.

Little Questions

Chaty killed herself in her Paris apartment,
surrounded by white lilacs.
Pierre continued to paint her
as if she were still alive.
Sometimes she's just a glint of white paint
in his wife's eye, at others
the long knob of a door pull
is the exact length of her nose.
Why is art so hard?
The sign on her door
said *back in an hour,*
the buzzer taped like a mouth.
A strand of hair caught under the tape.
Which happens often all over the world
accidentally every hour.
Because of the hair.
Yes, I think so now.
The sad blur of the hair crossing the tape.
A person can easily forget
how big seagulls really are
but not a single hair magnified under tape,
the strict manner in which it speaks.
Now is the time to get well.

Very quiet, hardly planning at all.
Look, a plate of eggs:
I don't have time to experiment
so I am eating them by myself
while they are still yellow.

Quick Note about
the Think Source

My dreams are not worth a halfpenny:
a battery cut in two, eighty orange roses,
an old boyfriend in a new car of the kind
he would never drive. Fortunately for us,
the universe is not that complicated:
eventually, words like *torpor* and *muddle*
came into being, and then torpid, muddled
accounts of the universe took over the populace,
many of whom died while it was snowing.
There is always someone willing to tell you
who they were, though it takes a little time
to find the professional, but much less than if
you had to do the reading yourself. If you are
planning on being born, you should know there was
a primordial abundance of helium, if something remains
in the same position for nine consecutive days
it is safe to assume it has passed, and that
oleanders really do grow along the Oxus,
which is a river. After that you are free to pursue
the violent activity of happiness. But for the universe,
after the first three minutes nothing of interest
occurred for 700,000 years: it just went on cooling

and expanding, as if it were asleep on a premium mattress,
until it felt cold enough to wake up and make stars.
The rest is almost history: volcanic holes, small
French paintings, one-eyed bats, a handwritten note
wedged between the doors of a church. And oh, one
more thing: when asked, if you say "I do not dance,"
the next day an infant is born without feet.

Kettle

I was washing the pot with my eyes closed,
running my hand over its surface,
searching for unacceptable bumps.
I kept telling myself perfectly clear minds
killed the Jews, yes, I said, the killers
were given advice, *stay calm, lean forward,*
do what you have to do with a clear mind.
And the Korean monks, life after life,
calm, forward, clear mind.
My posture was bad from bending over the sink.
I looked like someone who was going to spit.
How awful to be on all fours
when you met your death!
But mostly the evenings were calm.
Flat pond, tribunal of frogs,
lettuces growing in the turned earth,
a spade lying by in the half-greened grass,
and a baby duckling in the water
swimming behind his mother.
Why, there are six of them, they appear
to be gliding, it's positively depressing
we should try to be more like animals
and less like them at the same time.

Lullaby

My inability to express myself
is astounding. It is not curious or
even faintly interesting, but like
some fathomless sum, a number,
a number the sum of equally fathomless
numbers, each one the sole representative
of an ever-ripening infinity
that will never reach the weight
required by the sun to fall.
There is nothing on the ground
to pick up and examine.
It is too far back among the leaves
to reach. And here I am walking
idly, passing it from below,
with only a faint breeze to remind me
there is anything there,
the merest rustle of which
quiets me down to the point
I am able to sleep at all.

BIBLIOGRAPHY

MEMLING'S VEIL
(UNIVERSITY OF ALABAMA PRESS, 1982)

Standing Furthest, Transpontine, Replica

LIFE WITHOUT SPEAKING
(UNIVERSITY OF ALABAMA PRESS, 1987)

The Intended, From Memory, Patient Without
an Acre, All the Activity There Is, Barbarians

THE ADAMANT
(UNIVERSITY OF IOWA PRESS, 1989;
CARNEGIE MELLON UNIVERSITY PRESS, 2005)

Perfume River, At the North Pole, The Beautiful Is Negative,
The Last Supper, Pen and Ink, Depicted on a Screen,
Heaven on Earth, The Beginnings of Idleness in Assisi

APPARITION HILL
(CAVANKERRY PRESS, 2002; MS. COMPLETED 1989)

Lapland, Diary of Action and Repose, How It Is, Timberland,
Cul-de-sac, The Pedant's Discourse, Instrument of the
Highest, Naked Ladies, Toward the Correction of
Youthful Ignorance, Trust Me, Entirely, Eventually

COLD PLUTO

(CARNEGIE MELLON UNIVERSITY PRESS, 1996 AND 2001)

Nice Hands, Rain Effect, Cold Pluto, Out of a Hundred, Merengue,
Topophilia, Perpetually Attempting to Soar, Talking to Strangers,
The Brooch, The Cart, The March, Ancestors, The Butcher's Story,
The Hand, Minor Figure, Glory, The Wild Rose Bush

POST MERIDIAN

(CARNEGIE MELLON UNIVERSITY PRESS, 2000)

The Balloon, Perfect Reader, Tilapia, The Passing of Time, When Adults
Talk, Marked, Argosy, Sentimental Education, Chilly Autumn Evenings,
The Jewel, County Fair, The Letter, Pressed for Details, The Edge

AMONG THE MUSK OX PEOPLE

(CARNEGIE MELLON UNIVERSITY PRESS, 2002)

Furtherness, Thistle, Nothing Like the Earth, Full Moon, Silk Land,
Against the Sky, Mariposa and the Doll, Patina, Mercy, Among the
Musk Ox People, Seven Postcards from Dover, The Tragic Drama of Joy

TRISTIMANIA

(CARNEGIE MELLON UNIVERSITY PRESS, 2004)

The Great Loneliness, The Feast, Zettel, Japanese Bloodgod,
Magnificat, My Life as a Farmer (by James Dean), Critique of
Little Errors, Concerning Essential Existence, Do Not Disturb,
The Little I Saw of Cuba, In the Office of the Therapist I Behold
the Extinguished Guests, The Nutshell, Why I Am Not a Good
Kisser, Proscenium Arch, Oh Myrtie, From Here to Eternity

INDEED I WAS PLEASED WITH THE WORLD

(CARNEGIE MELLON UNIVERSITY PRESS, 2007)

A Picture of Christ, Gathered on a Friday in the Hour of Jupiter,
How I Became Impossible, The Tenor of Your Yes, My Happiness,
The Meal That Was Always There, Kiss of the Sun, Pontiac, My Timid
Eternity, Sweet Morning, The Imperial Ambassador of the Infinite,
After a Rain, Thirteen, Lines Written on a Blank Space, Little
Questions, Quick Note about the Think Source, Kettle, Lullaby

INDEX OF TITLES

AND FIRST LINES

Mary Ruefle has published ten books of poetry, a book of prose (*The Most of It*, Wave Books, 2008), and a comic book (*Go Home and Go to Bed!*, Pilot Books/Orange Table Comics, 2007); she is also an erasure artist, whose treatments of nineteenth century texts have been exhibited in museums and galleries, and published in *A Little White Shadow* (Wave Books, 2006). Mary is the recipient of numerous honors, including an Award in Literature from the American Academy of Arts and Letters, a Guggenheim fellowship, a National Endowment for the Arts fellowship, and a Whiting Award. She lives in Bennington, Vermont, and teaches in the MFA program at Vermont College.